UKE 'AN PLAY R...

Arranged by Hemme Luttjeboer

Alfred Publishing Co., Inc.
16320 Roscoe Blvd., Suite 100
P.O. Box 10003
Van Nuys, CA 91410-0003
alfred.com

ISBN-10: 0-7390-5421-X
ISBN-13: 978-0-7390-5421-5

Cover photographs:
Concert Crowd © istockphoto.com/dwphotos
"Flying V" Ukulele courtesy of Saga Musical Instruments

CONTENTS

AFTER MIDNIGHT

Words and Music by
JOHN CALE

Moderately fast rock

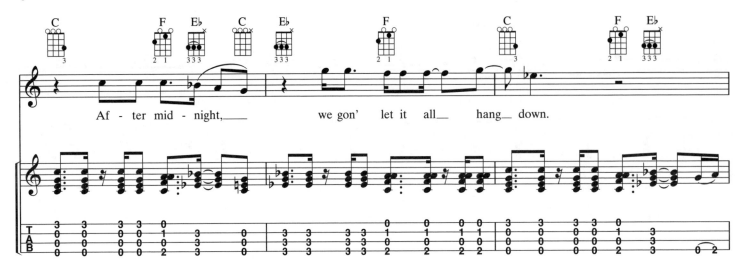

Af - ter mid - night,____ we gon' let it all__ hang__ down.

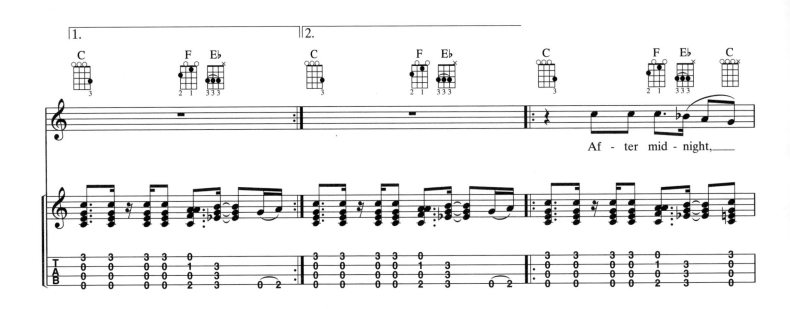

1.

2.

Af - ter mid - night,____

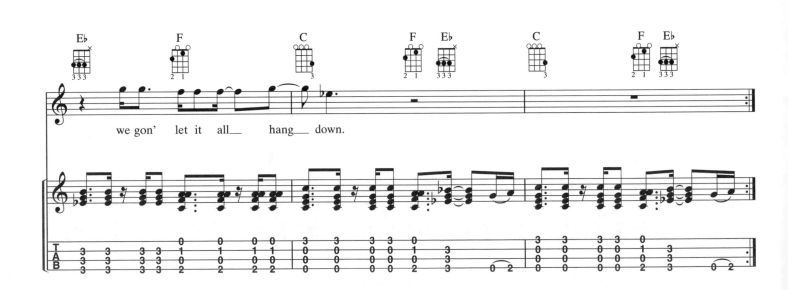

we gon' let it all__ hang__ down.

BAD COMPANY

Words and Music by
PAUL RODGERS and SIMON KIRKE

Tune down 1/2 step to match recording:
④ = G♭ ② = E♭
③ = C♭ ① = A♭

Bad Company - 5 - 1

AMERICAN IDIOT

Words by BILLIE JOE
Music by GREEN DAY

CHINA GROVE

Words and Music by
TOM JOHNSTON

China Grove - 5 - 1

Solo:

1.–5.   6.   *D.S. % al Coda*

Coda

CAT'S IN THE CRADLE

Words and Music by
HARRY CHAPIN and SANDY CHAPIN

Moderately fast ♩ = 75 with a 2 feel

Intro:

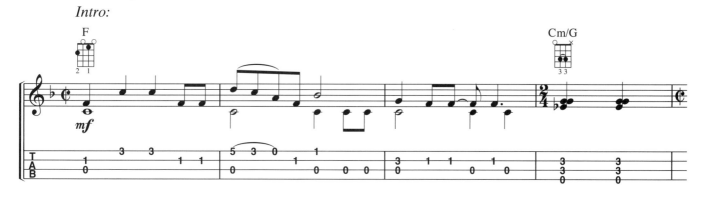

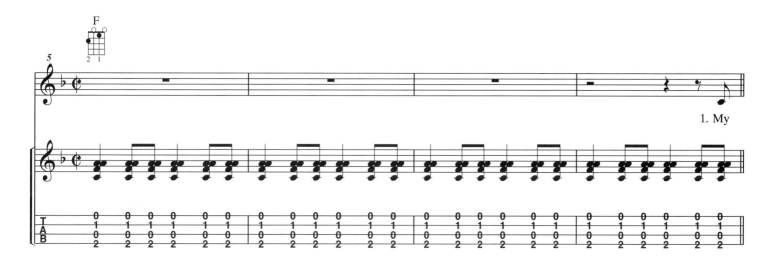

1. My

Verses 1 & 3:

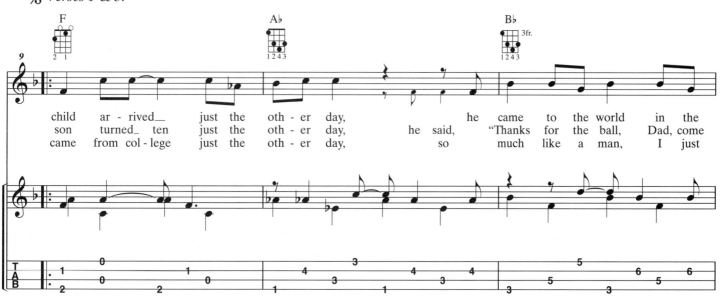

child ar- rived__ just the oth- er day,   he came to the world in the
son turned__ ten just the oth- er day,   he said, "Thanks for the ball, Dad, come
came from col- lege just the oth- er day,   so much like a man, I just

Cat's in the Cradle - 7 - 1

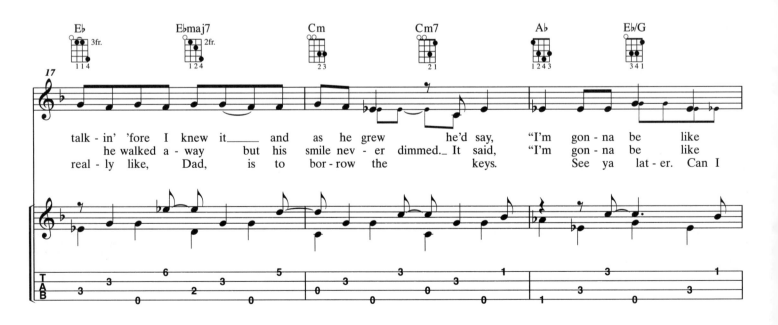

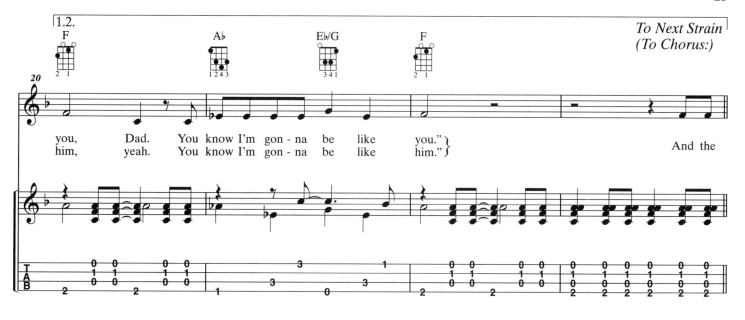

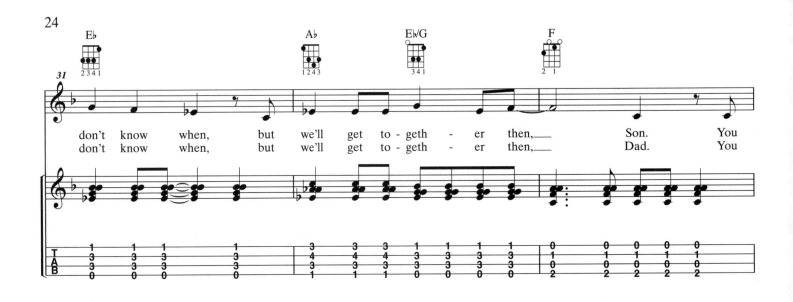

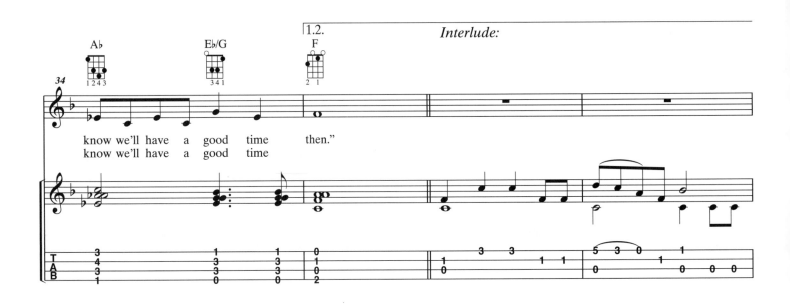

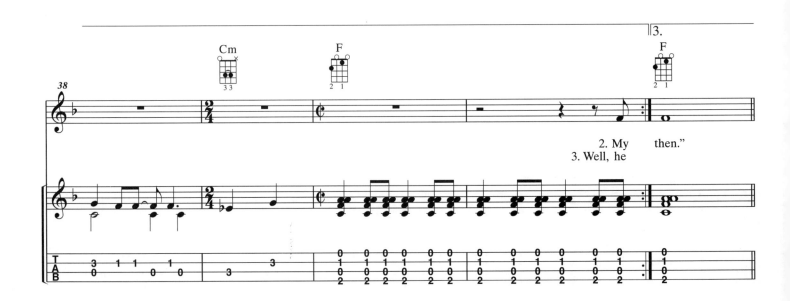

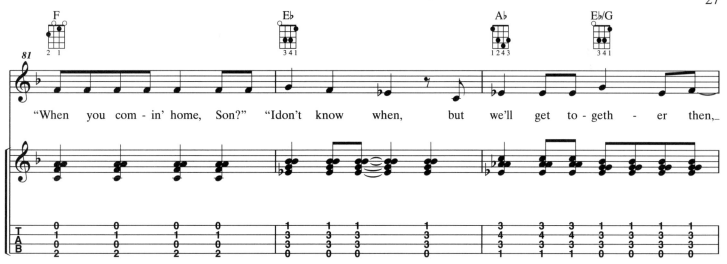

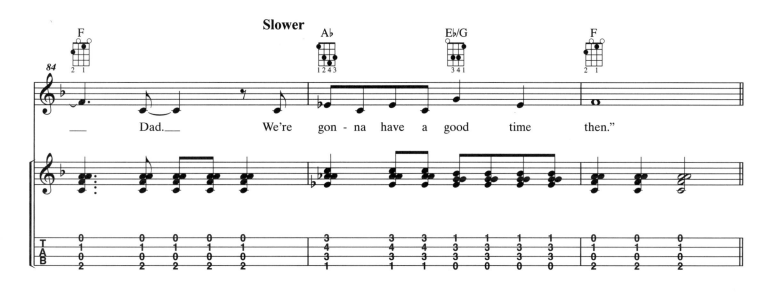

Outro:

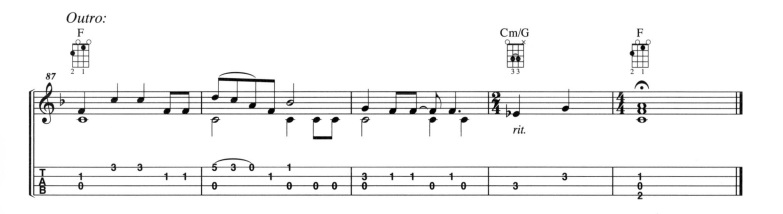

Cat's in the Cradle - 7 - 7

BOULEVARD OF BROKEN DREAMS

Words by BILLIE JOE
Music by GREEN DAY

Capo 1 to match record key.

Moderately fast ♩ = 86

Intro:

Verses 1 & 2:

1. I walk a lone - ly road, the on - ly one that I____ have ev - er known.__
2. I'm walk - in' down the line that di - vides me__ some - where in my__

___ Don't know where it goes, but it's home to me__ and I walk a - lone.__
mind. On the bor - der - line of the edge and__ where I walk a - lone.__

Cont. rhy. simile

I walk this emp - ty street on the bou - le - vard__ of bro - ken dreams,__
Read be - tween the lines, of what's f***ed up and__ ev - 'ry - thing's al -

Boulevard of Broken Dreams - 4 - 1

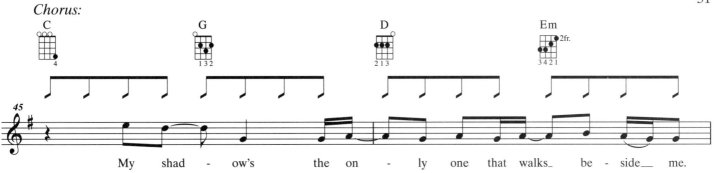

My shad - ow's the on - ly one that walks_ be - side_ me.

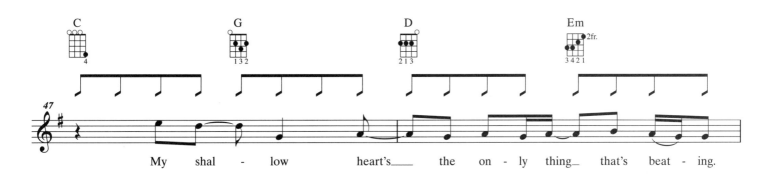

My shal - low heart's___ the on - ly thing_ that's beat - ing.

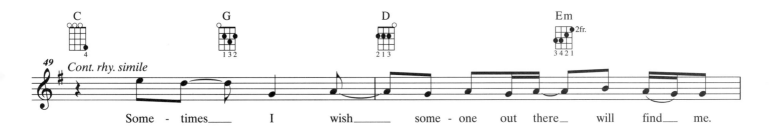

Some - times___ I wish___ some - one out there_ will find__ me.

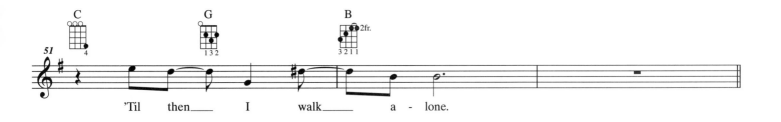

'Til then___ I walk___ a - lone.

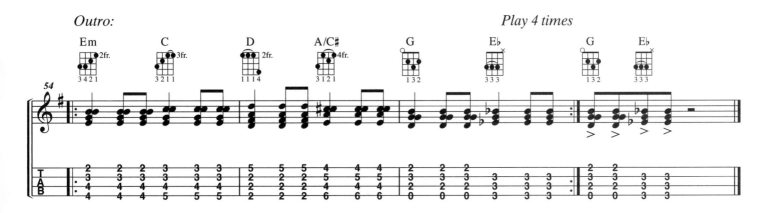

CLASSICAL GAS

By MASON WILLIAMS

Classical Gas - 4 - 1

Classical Gas - 4 - 2

Classical Gas - 4 - 4

FEEL LIKE MAKIN' LOVE

Words and Music by
PAUL RODGERS and MICK RALPHS

Moderately ♩ = 86

Intro:

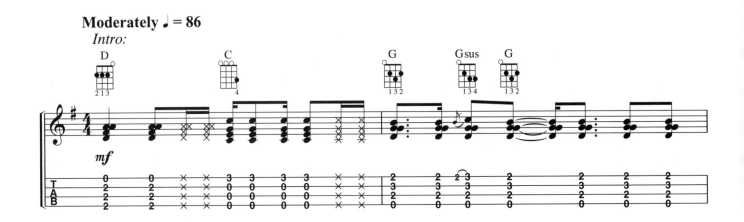

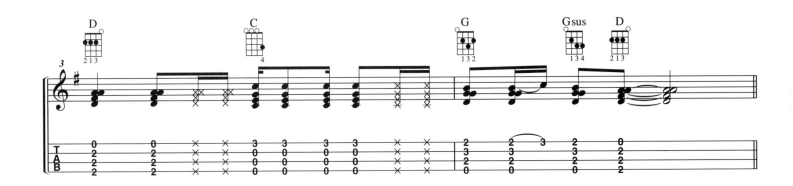

Verse:

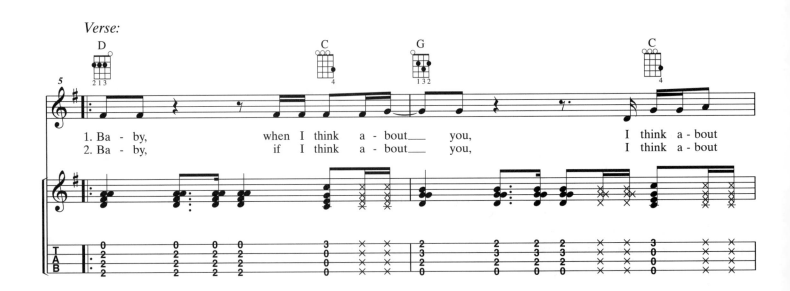

1. Ba - by, when I think a - bout___ you, I think a - bout
2. Ba - by, if I think a - bout___ you, I think a - bout

Feel Like Makin' Love - 5 - 1

Feel Like Makin' Love - 5 - 2

Feel Like Makin' Love - 5 - 5

FRIEND OF THE DEVIL

Words by
ROBERT HUNTER

Words and Music by
JERRY GARCIA and
JOHN DAWSON

Slowly in 2 ♩ = 162

Sec - ond one___ is pris - on, babe,___ sher - riff's on___ my trail. And

if he___ catch - es up___ with me,___ you know I'll___ spend my life in jail.

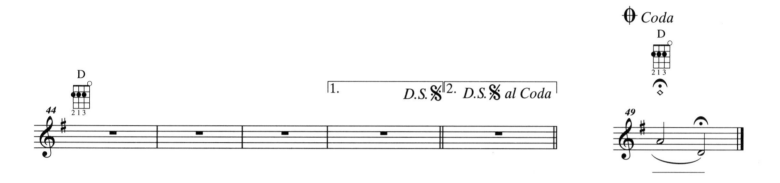

Verse 3:
I ran down to the levee,
But the devil caught me there.
He took my twenty-dollar bill
And vanishcd in thc air.
(To Chorus:)

Verses 4 & 6:
Got a wife in Chino, babe,
And one in Cherokee.
The first one says she's got my child
But it don't look like me.
(To Chorus:)

GOOD RIDDANCE (TIME OF YOUR LIFE)

Lyrics by
BILLIE JOE

Music by
BILLIE JOE and GREEN DAY

Bright in 2 ♩ = 86

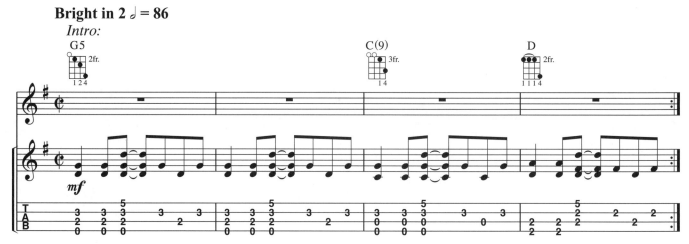

*For ease of use we have not used double noteheads for the unison G notes (open G and 3rd fret G).
Refer to the TAB for the correct fingerings.

1. An- oth- er turn- ing point, a fork stuck in the road.
2. So take the pho- to- graphs and still frames in your mind.
3. *Instrumental*

Time grabs you by the wrist, di- rects
Hang it on a shelf in good

Good Riddance (Time of Your Life) - 4 - 1

Good Riddance (Time of Your Life) - 4 - 2

Interlude:

Good Riddance (Time of Your Life) - 4 - 4

HEY THERE DELILAH

Words and Music by
TOM HIGGENSON

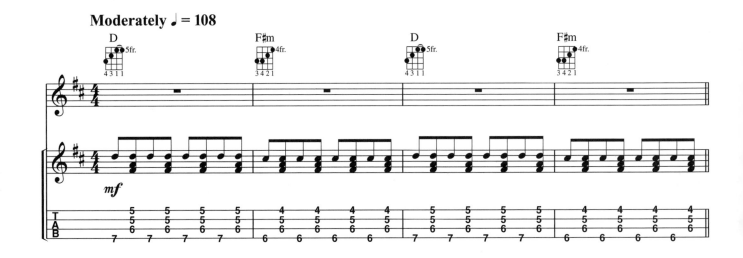

Verses 1 & 2:

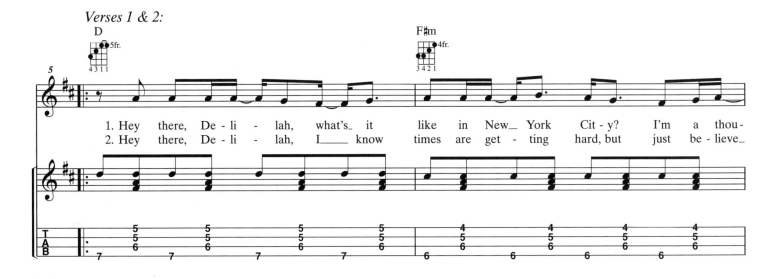

1. Hey there, De-li-lah, what's it like in New York Cit-y? I'm a thou-
2. Hey there, De-li-lah, I know times are get-ting hard, but just be-lieve

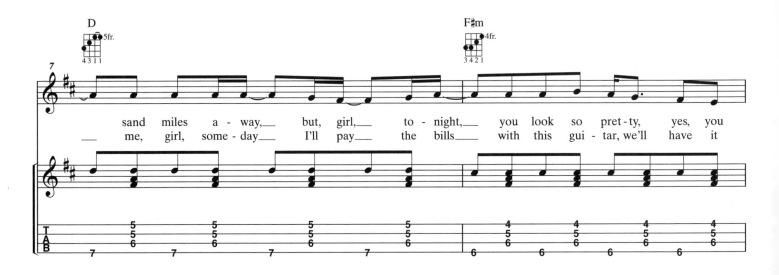

sand miles a-way, but, girl, to-night, you look so pret-ty, yes, you
me, girl, some-day I'll pay the bills with this gui-tar, we'll have it

Hey There Delilah - 6 - 1

Verse 3:

Cont. Verse patttern simile

A HORSE WITH NO NAME

Words and Music by
DEWEY BUNNELL

A Horse with No Name - 3 - 1

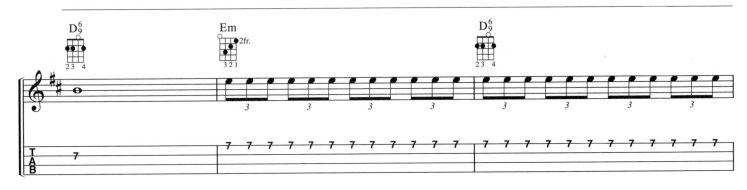

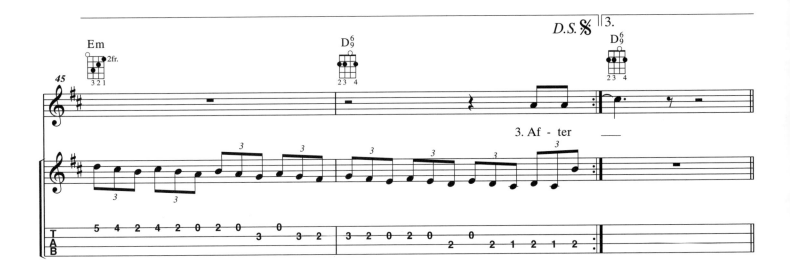

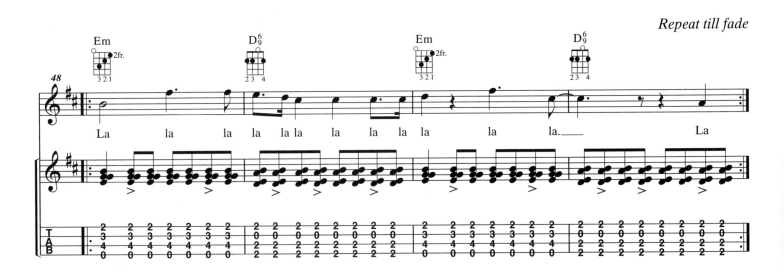

Verse 2:
After two days in the desert sun
My skin began to turn red.
After three days in the desert fun
I was looking at a river bed.
And the story it told of a river that flowed
Made me sad to think it was dead.
You see, I've…
(To Chorus:)

Verse 3:
After nine days I let the horse run free
'Cause the desert had turned to sea.
There were plants and birds and rocks and things,
There were sand and hills and rings.
The ocean is a desert with its life underground
And the perfect disguise above.
Under the cities lies a heart made of ground,
But the humans will give no love.
You see, I've…
(To Chorus:)

BEAT IT

Words and Music by
MICHAEL JACKSON

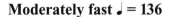

Tune down 1/2 step to match recording:
④ = G♭ ② = E♭
③ = C♭ ① = A♭

Moderately fast ♩ = 136

Intro:

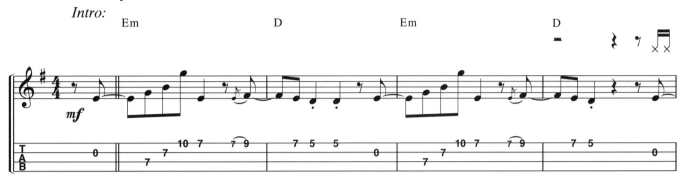

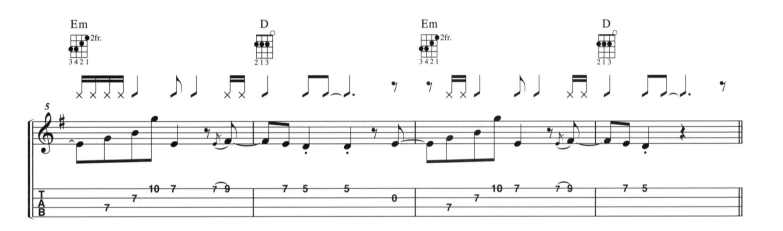

𝄋 *Verse:*

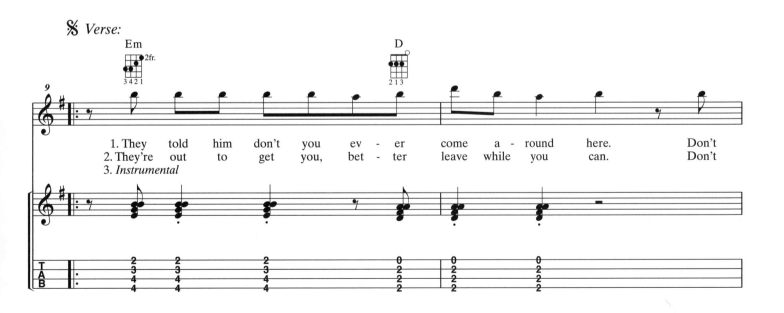

1. They told him don't you ev - er come a - round here. Don't
2. They're out to get you, bet - ter leave while you can. Don't
3. *Instrumental*

Beat It - 5 - 1

Interlude:

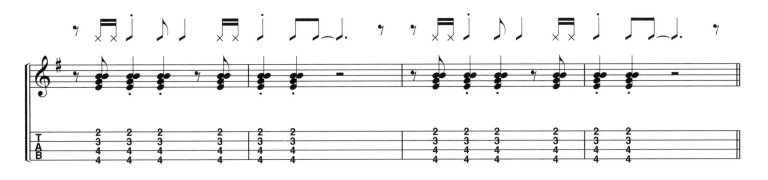

Coda

Outro Chorus:

Beat it,   beat it,   beat it,   beat it.   No___ one wants to be   de-feat-ed.   Show___

Play 4 times and fade

___ 'em how funk-y,   strong___ is your fight.   It___ does-n't mat-ter,   who's___wrong or right. Just

HOW YOU REMIND ME

Lyrics by
CHAD KROEGER
Music by
NICKELBACK

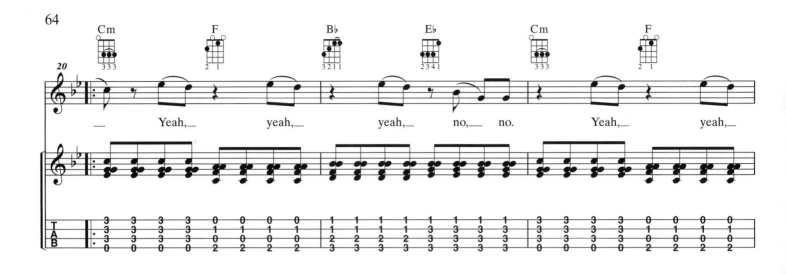

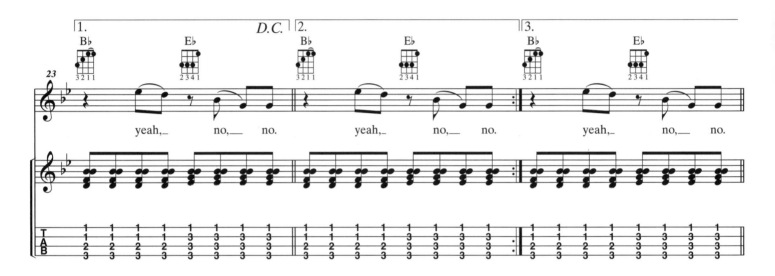

Interlude: sim. Intro:

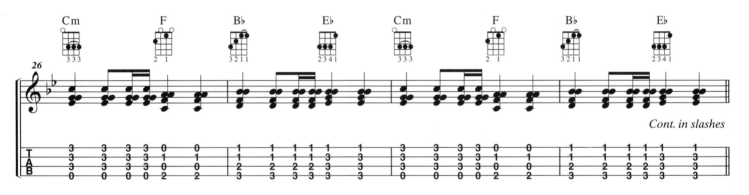

Nev-er made it as a wise man. I could-n't cut it as a poor man steal-in'. This is how you re-mind_

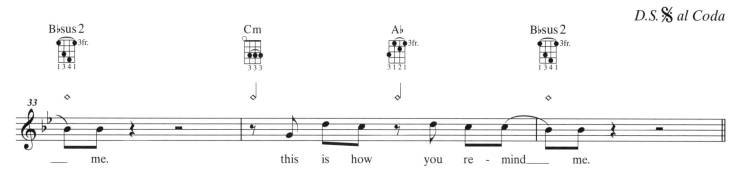

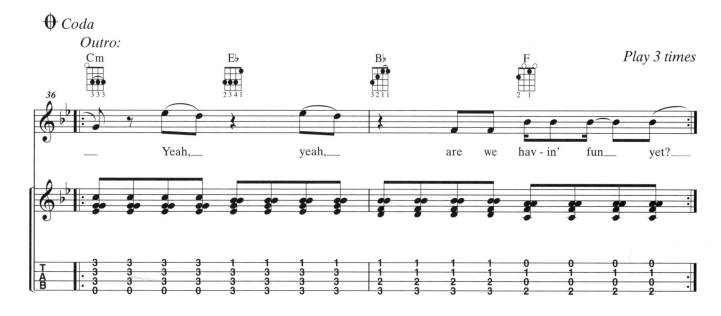

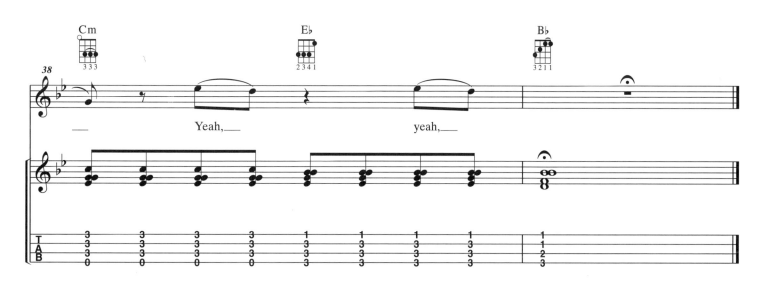

Verse 2:
It's not like you didn't know that.
I said I love you and I swear I still do.
And it must have been so bad.
'Cause livin' with me must have damn near killed you.
(To Chorus:)

BILLIE JEAN

Words and Music by
MICHAEL JACKSON

Moderately ♩ = 117

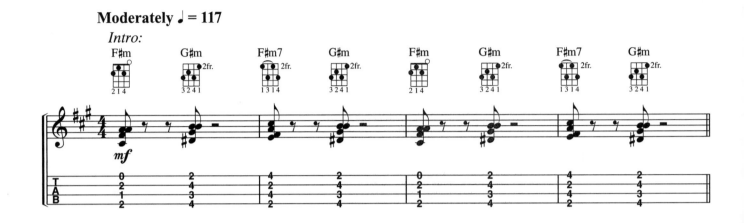

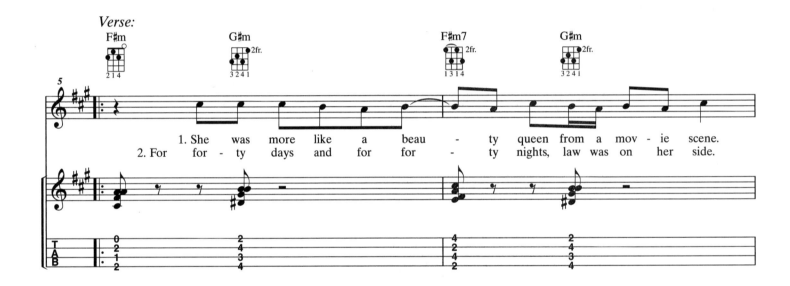

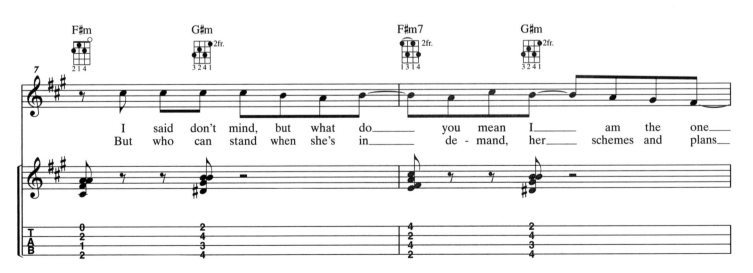

Billie Jean - 4 - 1

Billie Jean - 4 - 2

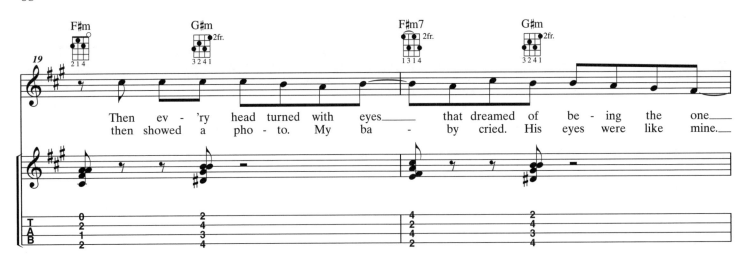

Then ev - 'ry head turned with eyes____ that dreamed of be - ing the one____
then showed a pho - to. My ba - by cried. His eyes were like mine.____

who will dance__ on the floor__ in the round.
Can we dance__ on the floor__ in the round?

Cont. in slashes

Bridge:

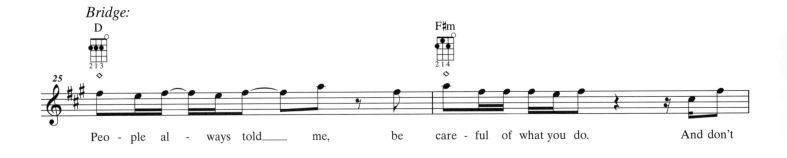

Peo - ple al - ways told____ me, be care - ful of what you do. And don't

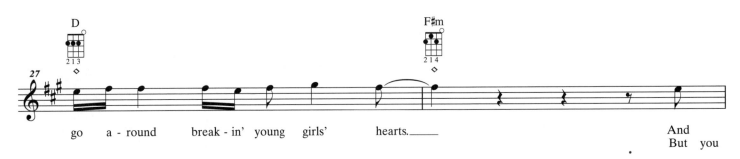

go a - round break - in' young girls' hearts.____ And
But you

Moth - er al - ways told me,___ be care - ful of who you love.
came and stood_ right by___ me, just a smell of sweet___ per - fume.

And be
This

care - ful of what you do___ 'cause the lie be - comes the truth. Hey.___
hap - pened much_ too soon.___ She called me to___ her room. Hey.___

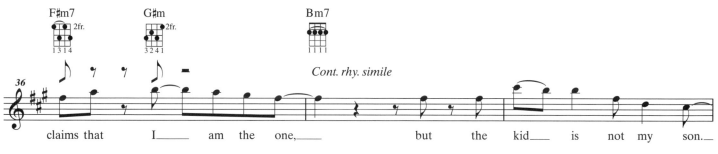

%̸ Chorus:

Bil - lie Jean___ is not my lov - er. She's just a girl___ who

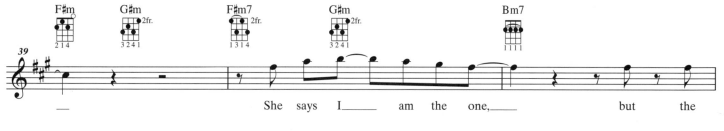

Cont. rhy. simile

claims that I___ am the one,___ but the kid___ is not my son.___

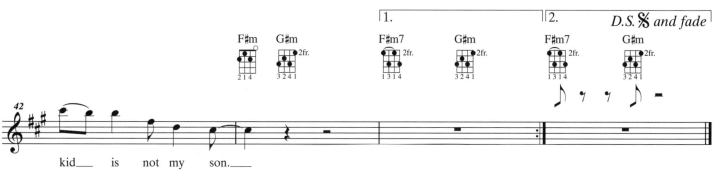

She says I___ am the one,___ but the

|1. |2. *D.S. %̸ and fade*|

kid___ is not my son.___

Billie Jean - 4 - 4

LONG TRAIN RUNNIN'

Words and Music by
TOM JOHNSTON

Moderately ♩ = 108

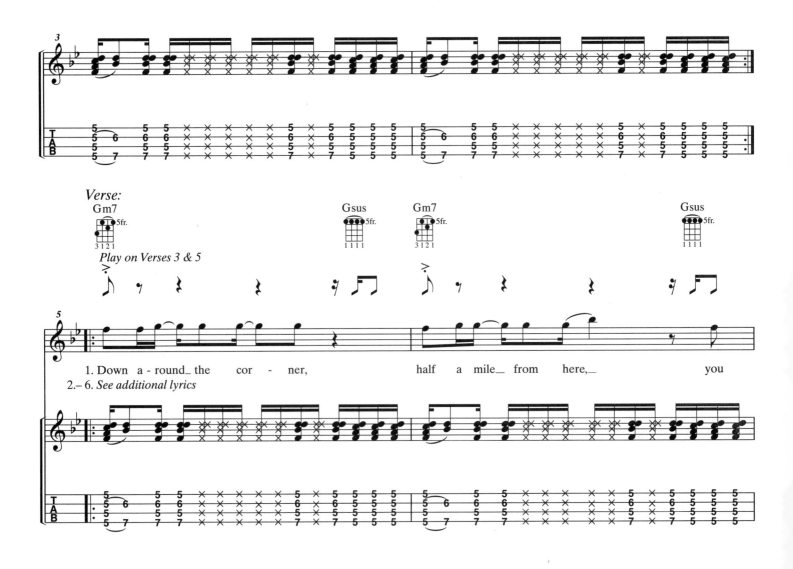

1. Down a-round the cor-ner, half a mile from here, you
2.–6. *See additional lyrics*

Long Train Runnin' - 4 - 1

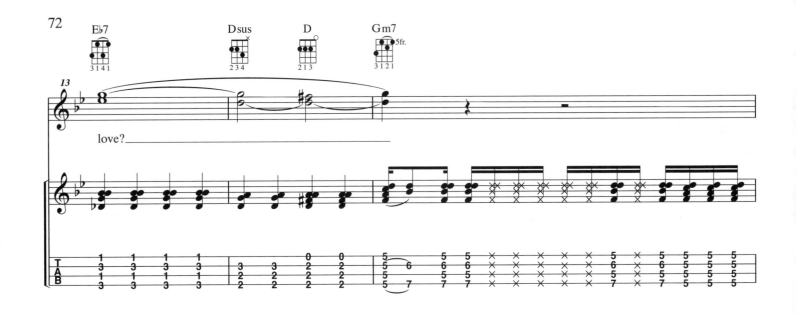

Outro:

Gm7

Repeat ad lib. and fade

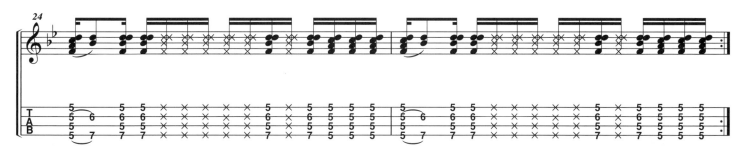

Verse 2:
You know I saw Miss Lucy,
Down along the tracks;
She lost her home and her family,
And she won't be comin' back.
Without love, where would you be right now,
Without love?

Verses 3 & 5:
Well, the Illinois Central
And the Southern Central freight,
Gotta keep on pushin', mama,
'Cause you know they're runnin' late.
Without love, where would you be right now,
Without love?
(1st time to Verse 4:)
(2nd time to Verse 6:)

Verse 4:
Harmonica Solo
(To Verse 5:)

Verse 6:
Where pistons keep on churnin'
And the wheels go 'round and 'round,
And the steel rails are cold and hard
For the miles that they go down.
Without love, where would you be right now,
Without love?
(To Coda)

MAMA TOLD ME NOT TO COME

Words and Music by
RANDY NEWMAN

To match original recording, Capo I

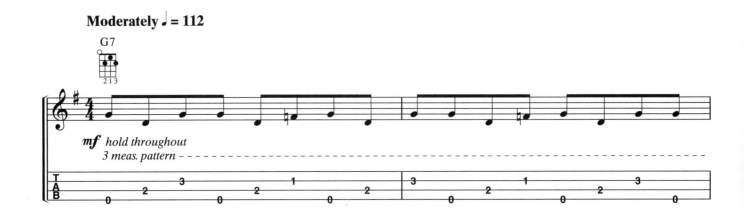

1. *Want some*

Verse:

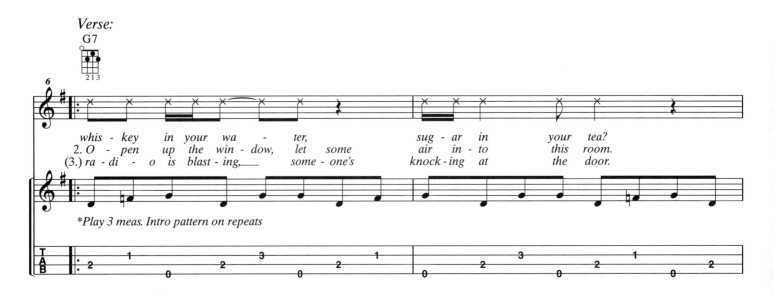

whis - key   in your wa   -   ter,   sug - ar   in   your   tea?
2. O - pen   up the win - dow, let some   air in - to   this   room.
(3.) ra - di - o is blast - ing,____ some - one's knock-ing at   the   door.

Play 3 meas. Intro pattern on repeats

*Note: The basic accompaniment pattern is a repeating 3-measure phrase that begins in the 8-measure Intro.
The 1st Verse starts on the 3rd measure of the 3-measure phrase. The 2nd Verse starts with the 1st measure of the
pattern and the 3rd Verse begins on the 3rd measure of the pattern (the pattern begins in the 3rd ending).

Mama Told Me Not to Come - 4 - 1

Mama Told Me Not to Come - 4 - 4

MR. BOJANGLES

Words and Music by
JERRY JEFF WALKER

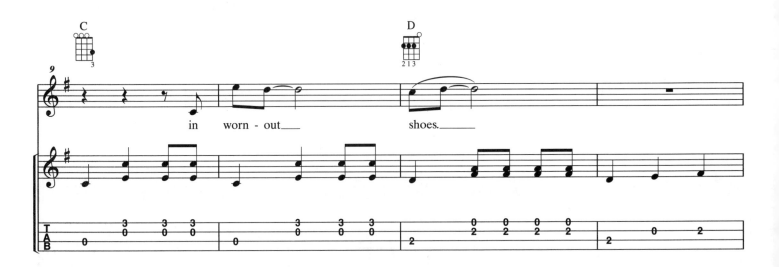

Mr. Bojangles - 4 - 1

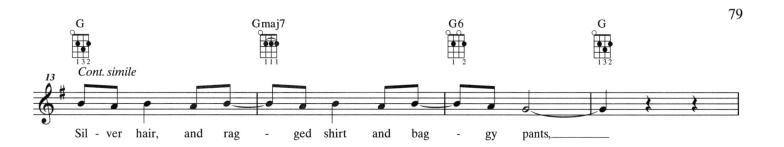

Silver hair, and rag - ged shirt and bag - gy pants,___

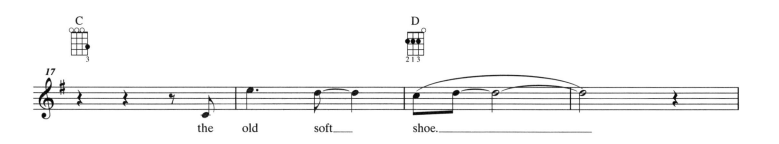

the old soft___ shoe._____

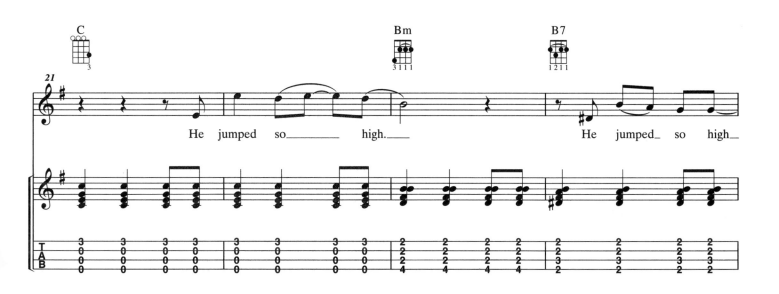

He jumped so_____ high.___ He jumped_ so high__

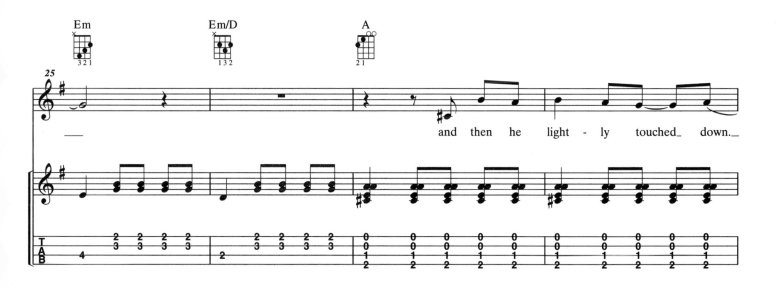

___ and then he light - ly touched_ down._

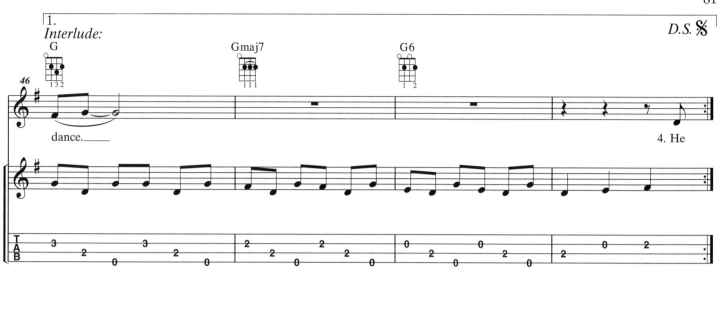

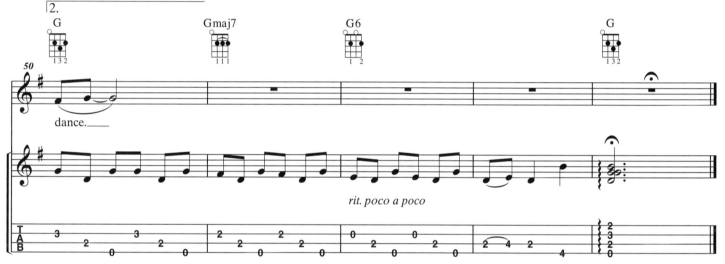

rit. poco a poco

Verse 2:
I met him in a cell in New Orleans.
I was down and out.
He looked to me to be
The eyes of age
As he spoke right out.
He talked of life.
He talked of life.
He laughed, clicked his heels and stepped.
(To Chorus:)

Verse 3:
He said his name, "Bojangles," and he danced a lick
Across the cell.
He grabbed his pants and spread his stance,
Woah, he jumped so high
And then he clicked his heels.
He let go a laugh.
He let go a laugh,
Shook back his clothes all around.
(To Chorus:)

Verse 4:
He danced for those in minstrel shows and county fairs
Throughout the South.
He spoke through tears of fifteen years,
How his dog and him
Travelled about.
The dog up and died.
He up and died.
After twenty years, he still grieves.

Verse 5:
He said, "I've danced now
At every chance in honky-tonk
For drinks and tips.
But most the time was spent behind these county bars
'Cause I drinks a bit."
He shook his head.
And as he shook his head,
I heard someone ask him, "Please, please"…
(To Chorus:)

OVER THE RAINBOW

(As performed by Israel "Iz" Kamakawiwo´ole)

Music by HAROLD ARLEN
Lyric by E.Y. HARBURG

Moderately ♩ = 84

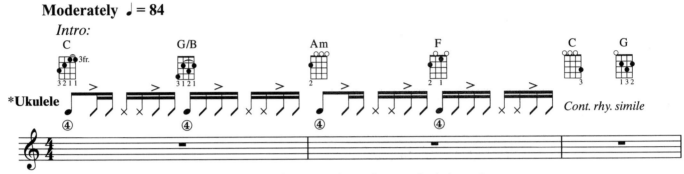

*Iz tunes his ukulele with the bottom "G" string tuned an octave lower than standard uke tuning.
You can play this arrangement with standard uke tuning. But, to get the sound of his bass lines
you will need a uke tuned GCEA—with a low G string.

Ukulele — Cont. rhy. simile

Oo, oo,_____ Oo, Oo,_____ Oo, Oo._____

Oo, Oo,_____ Oo, Oo._____

Chorus:

Cont. rhy. simile

Some - where o - ver__ the rain - bow,__ way__ up__ high.

Over the Rainbow - 3 - 1

blue - birds fly.
way___ up high.

And the dreams that_ you dare to,_ oh,

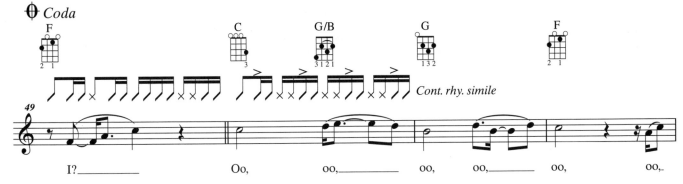

To Coda ⊕

D.S. 𝄋 *al Coda*

why, oh, why can't I,_____ I?_____ Some -

⊕ *Coda*

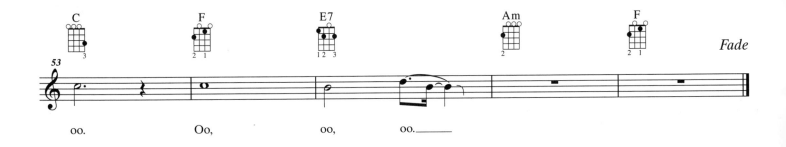

Cont. rhy. simile

I?_____ Oo, oo,_____ oo, oo,_____ oo, oo,_

Fade

oo. Oo, oo, oo._____

PETER GUNN

Music by
HENRY MANCINI

Moderately ♩ = 118
Intro:

A

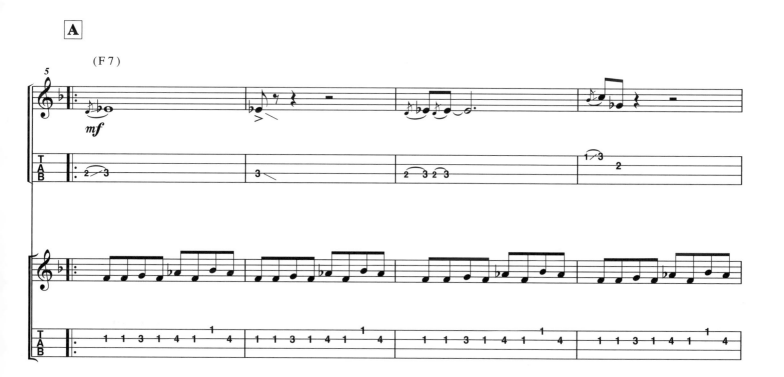

Peter Gunn - 3 - 1

Peter Gunn - 3 - 3

PEACEFUL EASY FEELING

Words and Music by
JACK TEMPCHIN

*Unison B notes played on strings 1 & 4.

1. I like the way your spark-lin' ear - rings lay
2.3. *See additional lyrics*
4. *Instrumental*

a - gainst your skin so brown.

And I wan - na sleep with you in the des - ert to - night,

with a bil - lion stars all a - round. 'Cause I got a

Peaceful Easy Feeling - 4 - 1

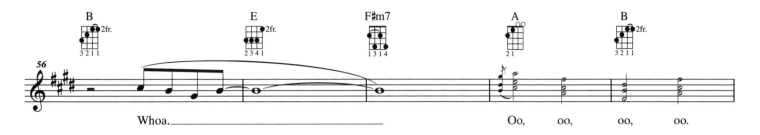

Whoa._____ Oo, oo, oo, oo.

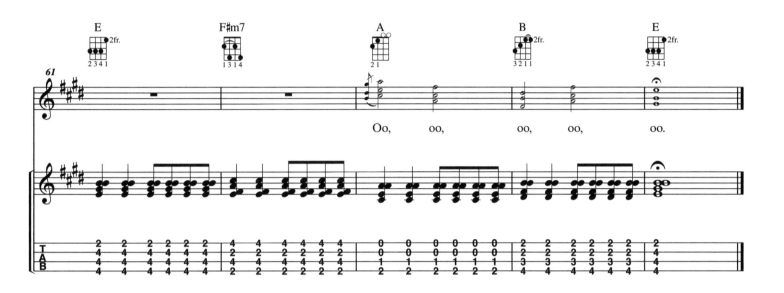

Oo, oo, oo, oo, oo.

Verse 2:
And I found out a long time ago
What a woman can do to your soul.
Ah, but she can't take you anyway,
You don't already know.
(To Chorus:)

Verse 3:
I get this feelin' I may know you
As a lover and a friend.
But this voice keeps whispering in my other ear,
Tells me I may never see you again.
(To Chorus:)

TAKE IT EASY

Words and Music by
JACKSON BROWNE
and GLENN FREY

Moderately ♩ = 138

Intro:

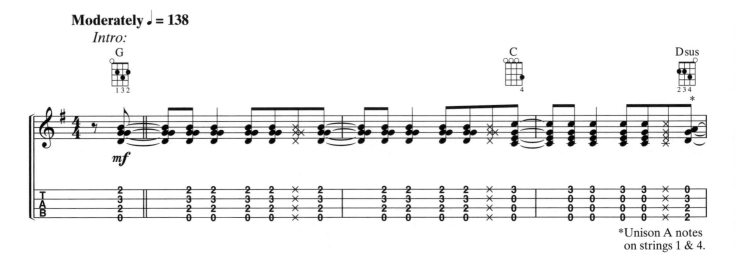

*Unison A notes
on strings 1 & 4.

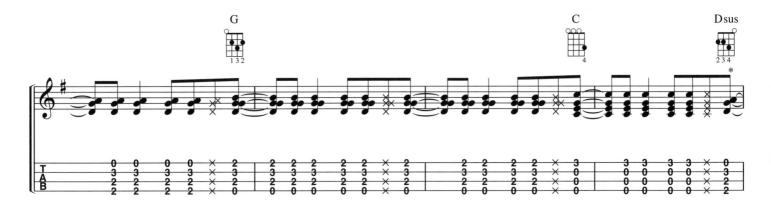

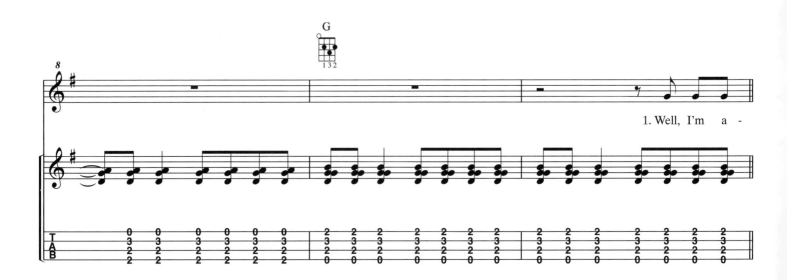

1. Well, I'm a -

Take It Easy - 5 - 1

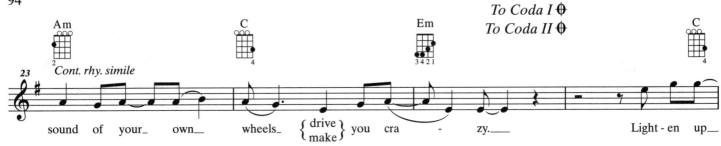

To Coda I
To Coda II

sound of your_ own_ wheels_ {drive/make} you cra - zy._ Light - en up_

_ while you still can,_ don't e - ven try_ to un - der - stand,_ just find a

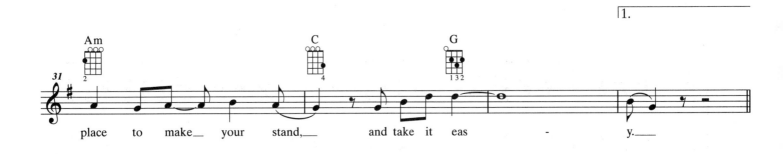

place to make_ your stand,_ and take it eas - y._

1.

2.

D.S. 𝄋 al Coda I
(To Instrumental)

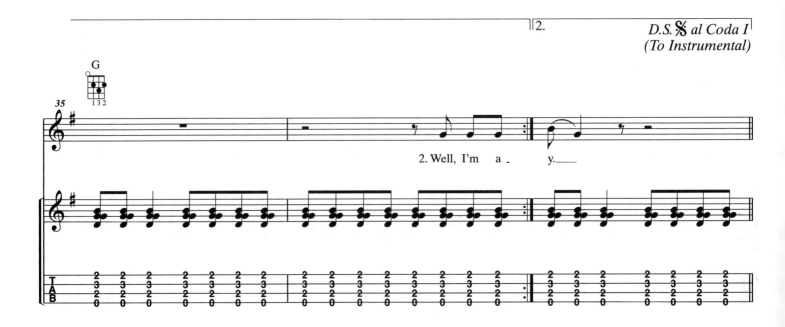

2. Well, I'm a _ y._

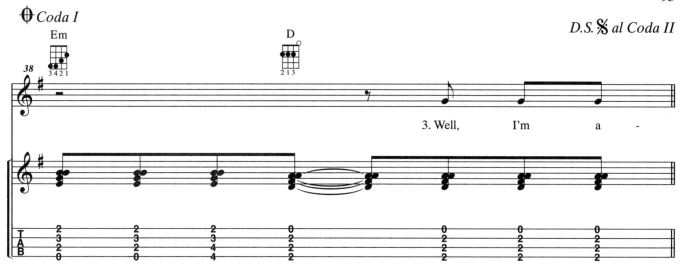

3. Well, I'm a -

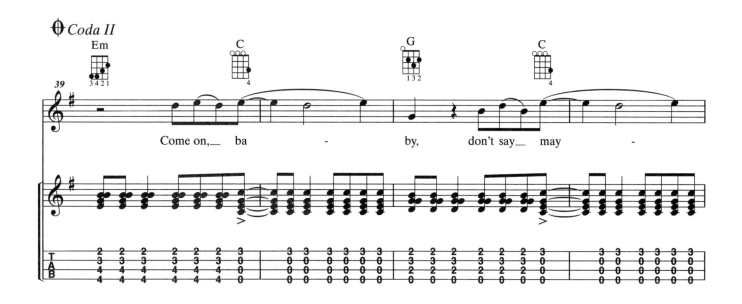

Come on,__ ba - by, don't say__ may -

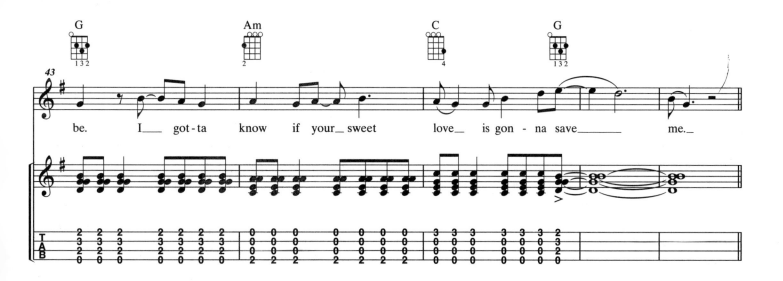

be. I__ got-ta know if your__ sweet love__ is gon - na save_____ me.__

Outro:

WILD NIGHT

Moderately fast ♩ = 152

Words and Music by
VAN MORRISON

*See TAB for riff played over the G chord throughout.

1. As you brush your

Bass line arranged for uke

Verse:

shoes walk by and stand be - fore_____ the mir -
girls dressed up for_____ each oth -

ror.
er.

And you comb your
And the boys

Wild Night - 5 - 3

100

Wild Night - 5 - 4

WAKE ME UP WHEN SEPTEMEBER ENDS

Words by
BILLIE JOE
Music by
GREEN DAY

Wake Me Up When September Ends - 4 - 1

YOU CAN LEAVE YOUR HAT ON

Words and Music by
RANDY NEWMAN

Moderate rock ♩ = 92

Intro:

Verse:

1. Ba - by, take off your coat____ real____ slow.
2. Go on o - ver there, turn on the light.
3. *See additional lyrics*

No, all the lights.

You Can Leave Your Hat On - 3 - 1

Verse 3:
Suspicious minds are talking,
Try'n' to tear us apart.
They say that my love is wrong.
They don't know what love is.
They don't know what love is.
They don't know what love is.
They don't know what love is.
I know what love is.